The Prince and the Wild Geese

Brigid Brophy

THE PRINCE
AND
THE WILD GEESE

St. Martin's Press
New York

First published in Great Britain by Hamish Hamilton.

Book design by Patrick Leeson

ISBN: 0-312-64551-1

First U.S. Edition

10 9 8 7 6 5 4 3 2 1

Printed in Hong Kong by
South China Printing Co.

1 A Female Cupid

IT WAS surely on the 14th of February, a saint's day of greater profane observance than sacred, that Julia Taaffe was presented with a sketch where the artist has poised her on the standard baroque cloud that, according to the Old Masters, transports divine apparitions to earth.

The year was 1832, the milieu the foreign colony at Rome.

Enchanting foreigners by its precocity, the Roman spring was cajoling girls out on expeditions to pick wild anemones and violets, which they carried home in nosegays through the streets. It signalled to the pious that Lent would arrive soon and to the boisterous that Carnival would arrive sooner. In everyone it stirred questions.

Which country would be invaded next by the impetus towards freedom that liberals named the March of Mind and the Duke of Wellington called the march of insurrection?

And whom would Julia Taaffe marry?

Sketching was in vogue. Foreign visitors stood long, until they looked like pillars themselves, in church and palazzo while they recorded in their notebooks the compositions of Old Master paintings. In regular bands, that might have been mistaken for bandits but for their bonhomie, they tramped out of Rome into the countryside, determined to demonstrate their susceptibility to Nature in pencil or watercolour.

Julia must have been given – and have lost – a score of keepsake drawings of the hills and rills outside Rome.

The picture she was given on the feast of Saint Valentine set itself apart from all that. Not only had its author a strong and pure feeling for colour. He was adept at drawing people.

There they most recognisably were, the men whose acquaintance Julia had made during her sojourn in Rome. And down they are going before her, pierced by love, collapsing in fiercely bloodied heaps like the wounded on a battlefield – though without detriment to the formality (as it must appear to a latterday eye) of their manners and dress.

Others step bravely up to challenge a wound; and one of them vaunts his invulnerability by wearing, over his fashionable modern dress, a breastplate.

Yet others flee, in undifferentiated dozens, from what is becoming an epidemic of infatuation with Julia.

They are diverse in nationality (the thicker-set being surely Swiss, German or English) and in mien. Some have what passes conventionally for a studious look (a matter, mainly, of spectacles). Some are men of the worldly world. The tall, burly one is notably similar to William Makepeace Thackeray (who, however, was spending that spring in London, though contemplating a trip to Italy, which in the event he postponed).

By curious accident, the sketch is a little in Thackeray's manner, both in technique and in its irony. The scratchy strokes match a certain satirical scratchiness of vision.

Gracefully, however, the artist includes, among the objects satirised, himself – or at any rate the comical completeness with which he has, literally, fallen in love.

All the same, he is using his skill as an act of wooing and he takes care to present himself presentably. His own is the most elegant of the figures, as well as the most grievously – the indeed mortally – wounded, as he lies flat on his handsomely clothed back with a love-arrow in his heart.

And Julia? Julia is merely touched-in, exiguously. Perhaps she dazzled the artist's eyes. Perhaps she lacked the repose that was the bonus virtue, for draughtsmen, in landscapes and altarpieces, with the result that even this adroit taker of likenesses could not capture hers until improving acquaintance licensed him (as it was to do in May) to ask her to keep still for a moment.

Yet, scarcely individualised though she is, Julia too is grazed with satire.

Defying standard iconography, the artist has invented a female Cupid. The real Cupid he reduces to a mere acolyte, a powder-monkey keeping her supplied with munitions.

In the rôle of Cupid Julia takes on not only some of the attributes but also the callousness of Diana the huntress. The outdoor setting, scene, probably, of flower gathering, becomes a field of carnage. 'Massacre of the innocents', says the artist's title for the picture in French (and his French uses the older spelling of *innocent* without the final *t*).

By the same device, Julia is made to take on responsibility. These victims are not succumbing to a third party, the god whose random mischief has to be excused on grounds of youth. They fall directly to Julia herself, by her intention and, pointedly, aim.

The picture adulates Julia but also accuses her: she wounds hearts for fun.

2 The Unreachable Rose

WHETHER BY the artist or by his art, Julia Taaffe was sufficiently touched (or amused, flattered or piqued) to keep the picture, together with others she received from the same hand.

Eventually, they were all mounted (probably by Julia herself, though the sequence is more haphazard than you might expect from someone who knew the context) in a ledger-like album, the front of which was stamped, in gold, 'Rome 1832'.

From Julia the album passed to a great-niece – or, at least, to someone who described Julia as her great-aunt but who may have been using the term in an approximate or honorary sense. Before bequeathing the album in her turn the great-niece provided some of the drawings with explanatory notes, not always of complete accuracy.

No doubt some of the flowers plucked in Rome that spring of 1832 were pressed and preserved in similar albums. And no doubt it was with the same unavailing wish to hold back that space of four or five months from oblivion that Julia kept the pictures that flowered from her suitor's hand and that he presented to her as both love letters and bouquets.

Romanticism itself was at springtime. So, many feared or hoped, was revolution. The spring Julia spent at Rome was in Britain a season of tenterhooks: would the House of Lords for the third time thwart the great Reform Bill and, if so, would agitation develop into revolution? Eighteen months earlier, in July 1830, the French, perhaps with a weary sense of having done it all before, had had a small revolution. They again dethroned a Bourbon but this time replaced him by Louis Philippe. The Papal States themselves, in whose territory Julia was staying, were not immune to the stir of freedom; in the spring of 1831 there had been an insurrection at Bologna.

Social revolution was not wholly distinguished, by opponents or practitioners, from nationalism. In 1830 the Belgians forcibly separated themselves from the Dutch. In 1831 the Poles rebelled against the Russians

but were defeated. Rebellion was perennially expected of the Irish.

About the time Julia reached Rome, Sir Walter Scott, Bt, thanks to whom the separate though not separatist culture of Scotland was the rage of Europe, arrived at Naples. (But his tour of milder climates did not restore his health. He went home to Scotland and died there in the September.) While Julia was slaying hearts at Rome, the opera season at Milan, which ran from Boxing Day 1831 to the end of Carnival 1832, included the first production of Vincenzo Bellini's *Norma*, an opera whose heroine, while she cannot be said quite to support, is certainly in sympathy with a nationalist rising against the imperialism of ancient Rome; and in April Gaetano Donizetti undertook to compose, by May, an opera about salves for hearts' wounds, *L'Elisir d'amore*. Julia danced and perhaps sang to the accompaniment of, in all likelihood, the pianoforte at which a prelude to Carl Maria von Weber's Konzertstück had been improvised, the year before, by the 21-year-old Felix Mendelssohn, a sojourner in Rome who applied himself seriously to sketching rural views and had just taken up working in sepia.

As the first precocious, southern roses of 1832 opened, Julia's draughtsman-suitor brought himself and his fellow-suitors even lower than he had laid them before Julia's arrows. This time his picture reduces them to caterpillars.

Julia, who evidently really did seldom keep still, is given the flittery wings of a fairy (by romantic iconography) or of Psyche (by classical) and has alighted in the position of the finest bloom: a sole virginal white flower on a tree of red roses, out of reach of the suitors who, in an explicit sexual metaphor, aspire to the position of the worm in the bud.

Julia herself perhaps felt like a flower squeezed in a social flower press.

---

3 *The Hero*

THE ELEGANT suitor-draughtsman was known to Julia, who conversed with him in French, as Prince Grégoire Gagarin and to his compatriots as Grigorii Grigorievich Gagarin.

As he made her his first bow, a purr of thunder ought, if there is any validity in poetic justice, to have rolled above Rome. It was an occasion to

satisfy the taste, endemic in that baroque city, for splendour and at the same time to gratify the yearning of the romantics for wildness. At the heart of Europe, source of the classical rules and the Catholic laws which had between them formed the culture of Europe, two people met who had severally come from Europe's most outlandish extremities, territories that had never been ingested into the ancient Roman empire nor yet, many considered, wholly tamed by modern civilisation either.

The Gagarin family claimed a common ancestry with the Russian monarchy. It could trace its lineage roughly back to the 9th century and in detail to the 15th. Its members were entered in the Fifth Book of the Nobility. From time to time official pronouncements confirmed new batches of Gagarin children, in the various branches of the family, as Princes of the Russian Empire.

Julia's suitor was born in 1810 in St Petersburg and was two when Russian arms and weather put Napoleon into retreat.

His father (also a Grigorii Grigorievich) was, after Waterloo, appointed Russian ambassador to Rome. In 1816, accordingly, he took up residence in Italy, and it was there that he brought up his children, Prince Grégoire *fils,* Prince André and Princess Anastasie.

The post-Waterloo society on which Gagarin *fils* exercised his talent for drawing people had taken on an appearance that was, suddenly, modern. The dividing line, which (at least after the death in 1830 of Sir Thomas Lawrence) put an end to grand portraiture in painting and condemned monumental portrait sculpture to a more lingering and lumpish decay, was the adoption by men of trousers – in which they could be elegant or worthy but not heroic. The defeat of Napoleon saved Europe from a nightmare (recurrent, as the Hundred Days of 1815 shockingly proved) but rendered it bereft of its last hero.

In the conviction that nothing would ever again be as exciting as Napoleon, Europe took up and cultivated, usually under the name *spleen,* the sensation of irritable boredom (which in the long run proved as fertile for literature as the sensation of the blues for popular music). In the same conviction, it adopted, probably from the example set by the works of Walter Scott, the notion that heroic events could happen only in 'history' (a secular counterpart to the vague supposition of Anglicans that miracles had no doubt taken place once upon a time, but not since the Reformation). Scott wrote a *Life of Napoleon* and in his novels usually pushed his heroes yet further back into history, beyond knee breeches and into doublet-and-hose or the kilt or some other form of skirt.

Gagarin occupied his young manhood in Rome as a student of art, though without the implication that he would ever need to earn his living as an artist – or, indeed, as anything. He was trained in the studio of Karl Pavlovich Bryulov (whose name is sometimes transliterated Briullov), a Russian painter some ten years his senior who, like Gagarin himself, had been born in St Petersburg but was now a long-term resident in Italy. In his middle age Gagarin published (in 1855) an appreciative memoir of Bryulov. It can scarcely, however, have been from Bryulov that the 22-year-old Gagarin had picked up the knack of satirising the unheroics of a trousered world which he employed to catch the attention of Julia Taaffe. During Julia's stay in Rome, Bryulov was at work there on a 21-foot picture, which it took him three years to complete. Walter Scott saw and admired it, unfinished though it presumably was. Edward Bulwer Lytton positively borrowed its subject and title for the novel he published in 1834, *The Last Days of Pompeii*.

Gagarin was not confined to the society of Russians in Rome. With his excellent French, he was scarcely less at home linguistically and probably more so spiritually in the circle of another painter.

The Académie de France had its Roman seat in the handsome Villa Medici, which stood, wrapped in gardens and a laurel shrubbery, on the slope of the Monte Pincio, with a view over the city to Saint Peter's and a convenient proximity to the Piazza di Spagna, where foreign visitors often stayed (and where one of them, John Keats, had died in 1821).

The small upper rooms of the Villa Medici provided uncomfortable bedrooms for 22 young Frenchmen, the winners of the annual competition in Paris for the Prix de Rome, which furnished musicians, architects, painters and sculptors with two years in Rome and an income for five years. The prize-winners ate communally in the refectory and went in for community singing, including what they chauvinistically called English concerts, where each of them sang a different tune in a different key – a discordancy that set the dogs howling on the Pincio and paid the perpetrators out for their chauvinism by giving French music a bad name among the shopkeepers in the Piazza di Spagna below. They painted and sculpted, sometimes in the Villa itself and sometimes in small studios distributed about the grounds, drank coffee and smoked in the Café Greco, lounged everywhere wearing slippers, straw hats and blouses splattered with plaster, kept big dogs, and grew their hair and side whiskers but chopped them down for fear of reprisals when their bohemian appearance led the Romans to suspect that France was again exporting revolution.

The director of the Académie, now in his early forties, was Horace Vernet, a painter who specialised in battle pieces but was of an exceptionally kind disposition. Vernet escaped the prevailing post-

Napoleonic tristesse by remaining a bonapartist and by virtue of the huge energy with which he, very rapidly, painted. He and his wife, whom Mendelssohn considered 'the kindest creature in the world', exercised a shared vocation for making people feel at home at the Villa Medici.

Their immediate household there consisted of their daughter Louise, who played the piano and, when she became excited at parties, the tambourine; Horace Vernet's father, Carle Vernet, himself a painter of horse pictures and of battle pieces that had won Napoleon's approbation, and evidently the originator of the family energy, since, at 72, he still rode daily and often danced the quadrille all evening; and Horace Vernet's two dogs.

The couple's parental talent and good will, however, encompassed also the students whose administrative good order was Horace Vernet's responsibility and to whom he was friendlily known as 'Monsieur Horace', and it reached out to other foreigners in Rome, including, in the spring of 1831, Mendelssohn and, in the following spring, Prince Grégoire Gagarin.

It was surely at the Villa Medici, under the auspices of Horace Vernet, that Gagarin met Julia Taaffe – probably at one of Madame Vernet's regular Thursdays, where students and 'society' mixed. It was Horace Vernet's warlike subject-matter that Gagarin turned to satirical and love-making purpose when he depicted the Thursday population of Madame Vernet's drawing room going down in wounded heaps before Julia. And after training under Bryulov, Gagarin was bound to take pleasure in the speed with which Vernet executed his pictures.

Vernet was, indeed, proud of it himself. When Mendelssohn, improvising for him at the pianoforte more usually played by his daughter, moved on from Weber themes to themes from Mozart's *Don Giovanni* because he knew that to be Vernet's favourite music (especially the arrival of the Commendatore at the end – perhaps because he arrives in armour), Vernet repaid the compliment by confessing that he too was an improviser, preparing a canvas and dashing off a portrait of Mendelssohn.

A year later he did a portrait (this time a lithograph) of Gagarin. Julia Taaffe kept a copy of it along with the drawings by Gagarin himself, and it is pasted, like a frontispiece, into the beginning of the album.

Julia's great-niece explained it, in the note she wrote to accompany it, as a portrait of Gagarin 'in fancy dress'. It is impossible now to know whether Gagarin went, thus attired, to a fancy dress ball at the Villa Medici or perhaps took part there in amateur theatricals or whether it was Horace Vernet who picked on something heroic in his elegant young guest's demeanour and whisked him into an appropriately 'historical' costume for his portrait.

Vernet's studio, which was in one of the detached buildings in the Villa gardens, might well have been equipped to dress Gagarin up on the spur of the moment, since (as well as housing a pet monkey) it was full of the properties (especially guns) that modelled for the incidental details in Vernet's pictures.

In any case, there Gagarin stands, looking perhaps as he wished Julia to see him: handsome, at ease but on the right side of arrogant, and in a costume he no doubt considered more suited than modern dress to the rapture of his love for her. Not for an instant, however, can he be mistaken for someone actually living in the 16th century, so cardinally does he incarnate a vision of history from across the gulf left by Napoleon. Indeed, he might be a character from an opera first performed, at Naples, three years before Vernet drew his portrait, Donizetti's *Elizabetta al castello di Kenilworth,* whose libretto Andrea Tottola had adapted from Walter Scott's novel *Kenilworth*.

As though he truly were a character from an Italian opera or had prevailed on Julia to see him as one, Julia's copy of the lithograph bears the pencilled name 'Grigorio' (though the usual Italian form of the name is Gregorio).

---

4 *Choice of Partners*

IF THERE was ever a gap in the circle of men about her, Julia Taaffe may, during one of the evening parties at the Villa Medici in late January or early February 1832, have glanced up and seen, advancing across Horace Vernet's drawing room, a figure she might have taken for the ghost of Napoleon.

Golden foliage marched, in brocaded files, up the front and round the stiffened, stand-up collar of his uniform – which, however, bulged over his portliness. He talked in the decisive, incisive manner of an emperor dispensing mercy or doom. He complained, even as he stood in the middle of it, that society in Rome was boring and backward. He defined, with the precision of the Code Napoléon, the opposition between Classicism and

Romanticism. Even when, taking advantage of the mildness of the Roman evening, Vernet opened the doors and led him onto the balcony and hence displayed Rome beneath, moonlit, the dome of Saint Peter's a black silhouette, a sight that as a rule took visitors' breath away, he talked on, omnicompetently disparaging the present condition of music, the theatre and the visual arts and maintaining to Vernet's face, which never the less remained dignified and friendly, that the Vernet style of painting was reactionary and must be swept aside.

What most made him seem a middle-aged resurrection of the Emperor was the impression he gave, which everyone seemed to recognise, of genius, together with an impression, unlocatable but no less universally apparent, of vulgarity.

The grand uniform was in fact that of the French consular service. The plump ghost will have been presented to Julia as Henri Beyle, the French Consul at Civitavecchia, the coastal town that served Rome as its port. He possessed, however, as well as genius, the one quality that could rival Julia's sexual attractiveness for drawing power in a drawing room, celebrity. He trailed clouds of women whispering the explanation that, under the name Stendhal, the Consul was the famous author of *Le Rouge et le Noir.*

For his part, he is sure to have decorated his bow to Julia with a felicitation on her good luck in being a compatriot of Shakespeare. He will not have listened to her disclaimer but will have turned to Horace Vernet and recounted to him the argument of the pamphlet he had published a decade before, *Racine et Shakespeare,* in which the two dramatic poets stood for, respectively, Classicism and Romanticism.

By the 14th of February, however, as Gagarin was both classically and romantically transforming Julia into Cupid, the consular ghost had, as reluctantly as the ghost of Hamlet's father at the paling of the glow-worm's fire, stalked back to Civitavecchia, which he considered even more tedious than Rome, and Julia was having to repeat her disclaimer to other interlocutors.

They very likely included Hector Berlioz, one of the Prix de Rome winners living at the Villa Medici. He was now 29; his music and his politics were alike reputed to be revolutionary and in both cases as unruly as his shock of red hair. Spleen, by which he was often attacked, cannot for ever have held him back from expounding to Julia his passion for the plays of Shakespeare, in expression of which he had composed overtures to *The*

Rome. Février 1832. 1836

Tempest and *King Lear* and thought of composing a scherzo on the Queen Mab speech in *Romeo and Juliet*, though he was afraid of being beaten to the execution of the project by the friend and fellow-Shakespearean he had mentioned it to during a ride in the Campagna, Mendelssohn.

Julia may well have been surprised to learn that what Berlioz admired about Shakespeare was his wildness, since, in her own probable acquaintance with them, his plays no doubt seemed, on the contrary, rather tame and trite – reduced as they were to a few contextless morsels apiece, each under its sententious editorial heading ('The Justice of Providence' and 'Patience and Sorrows' representing the pith of *King Lear* and 'Rural Simplicity' of *The Winter's Tale*), in the poetry volume (companion to its prose predecessor) of *Elegant Extracts* ('Selected for the Improvement of Young Persons').

Julia had cause to disclaim, perhaps indignantly, being English. She was, as she made clear to Gagarin and he reflected in the title of one of his pictures, Irish.

In traceable lineage, the Taaffe family (whose members thus spelled themselves and were spelt by genealogists, though Julia's great-niece accorded them only one *f*) fell only a few centuries short of the Gagarins. The family was, according to the account the ninth Viscount Taaffe wrote in 1856, 'of great antiquity and considerable repute in the counties of Louth and Sligo' and had 'produced many eminent persons', the earliest recorded of whom were a Sir Richard and a Sir Nicholas Taaffe, who owned land in Co. Louth in the 13th century.

One of Nicholas's descendants was created first Viscount Taaffe in 1628. In the next generation, however, a Taaffe was already shewing signs either of wanderlust or of discontent with Ireland and was pursuing a military career in the service of the Austrian Empire.

By the early 18th century, that perhaps inherent Taaffe tendency had been reinforced by the disabilities imposed by Parliament on Papists, which most of the Taaffes, including Julia, were. Catholics were excluded from the Dublin Parliament, from high military rank, from the learned professions and in some circumstances from land-owning – from, that is, virtually the only occupations that the top branch of the Taaffe family would have considered fit for its members.

Accordingly, a whole segment of the family broke away and became authentic wild geese, as the Irish migrants to the continent of Europe called themselves, serving the Austrian (or Holy Roman) court as soldiers and diplomatists.

To their Anglo-Irish viscountcy they added, in 1758, the title of Count of the Holy Roman Empire. Indeed, the foothold these migrants took on Austro-Hungarian-Bohemian territory was prehensile. They acquired a Schloss in Bohemia. They made it their custom to marry into the Austrian,

Germanic and Balkan nobilities, whose names and titles jingle half ludicrously, half musically as though their owners were taking a sleigh-ride while wearing their jewelled and enamelled orders. Thus the ninth Viscount Taaffe, who was known in Austria as Lord Lewis Taaffe, had in 1822 married Princess Amalia, Dame of the Starry Cross, daughter of their Serene Highnesses Prince Bretzenheim von Regécz and Princess Maria Walburga Josefa of Oettingen-Oettingen and Oettingen-Spielburg.

Yet the wild geese Taaffes retained the nostalgia of migrants. Their given names were cosmopolitan assemblies in which Ireland was not forgotten. The ninth Viscount (who was also the fourth Count of the Holy Roman Empire) bore the names Lewis Patrick Johann. When he had his history of his family privately printed in Vienna, it was (which caused the printer palpable difficulties) in English.

The passage of more than a century and the removal of most of the disabilities did not diminish either the indignation or the legalistic pedantry of his argument that the penal disabilities imposed in the reign of Queen Anne had betrayed the promises made to the Irish Catholics after the Battle of the Boyne in 1690.

No more had the Bohemian Schloss displaced older images in his mind's eye. He illustrated his book with engraved pictures of the tumbledown castles in Ireland, that can have been neither beautiful nor comfortable in the first place, of which his family had been dispossessed.

Julia belonged to the section of the family that had, with a few defectors here and there, stayed in Ireland. Her father, John Taaffe, had his seat at Smarmore Castle, Co. Louth – which was presumably a bit less of a ruin than the castles delineated in his Austro-Irish kinsman's book, since it had to accommodate the fourteen children of his two marriages.

Of those children, Julia, who was born in 1806 (and was thus some four years older than Gagarin), was the youngest.

Her mother, who was also a Taaffe (from Co. Meath), had died in 1825, barely a fortnight after the death of her husband, thereby orphaning a family of, in the main, unmarried girls.

It must have been clear to everyone, Julia herself included, with what purpose Julia and her immediately elder sister were sent to Rome in 1832.

As spring advanced, parties and dances multiplied. Hosts and guests wanted to enjoy as many as possible before the Lenten embargo, which would mute parties and outlaw dances altogether.

Julia found herself with an ever greater choice of dancing partner – that is, behind the transparent pretexts of the conventions, of husband.

In February, Grégoire Gagarin drew a picture of her at the centre of a figure in a country dance, looking pert and playing eeny-meeny-miny-mo, as it were, among potential partners.

He is, as usual, accusing her of flirtation – perhaps with more than usual bitterness, since the potential partners do not include himself. (Was it that he could not, despite the evident polish of his manners, dance? Or was it that he would not, feeling some Byronic lameness in his soul?)

Yet his picture also shews her, for once in repose, remembering the scene afterwards; and he is not unaware of or indifferent to her true perplexity.

For all the comedy of Gagarin's touch and their own lightness of heart, if not of foot, the prancing figures hint at the monstrous. They are as uncertain of temper as dancing fauns. As they encircle Julia, they hold her captive. They are agents of social and economic stringency, closing in, to press her to a decision.

She, perhaps, is hesitating not only between one suitor and the next but between the opposite promptings of the Taaffe inheritance: love of Ireland; and the adventurousness of the wild geese.

Were she to marry Gagarin, whose ambassador father would sooner or later be recalled, how distant and irrecoverable must Smarmore Castle look from St Petersburg.

5 *The Taaffe Girls*

THE FATE of girls, the great theme of the novels of Jane Austen which were published in the second decade of the century, was a preoccupying responsibility not only to themselves but to the fathers and brothers who were (or by survival became) heads of families – and also to grandees, who often undertook a protective responsibility towards large extended families of portionless kindred and dependants.

The socially acceptable occupations open to a well-born woman in 1832 were even fewer than those open to a well-born Irish Catholic man a century earlier. Julia could study examples of most of the options, such as they were, among her sisters.

The children of her father's first marriage consisted of two daughters, both of whom married, at home in Ireland, before Julia was born.

Her father's second marriage produced, first, a son, who was named John like his father. The ensuing children consisted of three further sons and eight daughters.

To Julia's eldest brother it fell first to share and presently to inherit the responsibility for his eight girl siblings, though two of the eldest early removed themselves, one by marrying and the other by taking the most stringent of the options and becoming a nun.

Such provision as John Taaffe *fils* could make for the rest of his sisters was largely by way of his own marriages. Again like his father, he married twice.

His first marriage was Irish, and it created a connexion that was instrumental in Julia's visit to Rome.

His second was made positively on Roman territory – in, that is, the Papal States. His wife, herself a widow (of the Marchese Gabucini), was the daughter and heir of an Italian Count from Fano.

It was no doubt thanks to their eldest brother's Italian marriage that one of the Taaffe girls, Anne, married Count Luigi Borgogelli, also of Fano in the Papal States. And no doubt it was Anne's example that the two youngest Taaffe girls were expected to emulate during their sojourn on Papal territory.

Exactly which of her sisters it was who accompanied Julia to Rome is in doubt. Writing an explanatory note to Grégoire Gagarin's picture of the sisters, their great-niece called them 'Our Great Aunts, Joanna & Julia Taafe' (*sic*). However, although Julia's sisters were numerous enough to offer considerable diversity of names, there was not in fact a Joanna among them. Julia's immediately nearest siblings were, in ascending order, Martha and Frances, both of them born in 1802 – presumably, since they are not recorded as twins, one at each extremity of that year.

Yet it seems unlikely that a great-niece, even a perhaps merely honorary great-niece and even one who could misspell her great-aunt's surname, would be utterly mistaken about that great-aunt's first name – which must have been, after all, the name by which she addressed her and heard her spoken of in the family.

Conjecture, therefore, is entitled to step in and suggest that Julia's companion in Rome was Martha and that, while she was abroad and conveniently removed from most of the people who had known her all her life as Martha, she intimated that she wanted to be known henceforth as Joanna.

An immediate reason for discarding the name Martha was very likely provided in Rome. In a cosmospolitan society, Taaffe must have constantly been pronounced as two syllables, with either a wide Italian or a slurry German *e* at the end. Indeed, the sisters probably met people, either from

Austria itself or from the Austrian domains in Italy, who knew of their powerful (and no doubt there disyllabic) Taaffe kinsman in Vienna. When the two girls appeared independently in society, the elder could camouflage herself as Miss Taaffe *tout court*, but since they were known to have older unmarried sisters at home she must sometimes have had to answer to Miss Martha Taaffe – which, if the final *e* of Taaffe was pronounced, made a jangle anyone would want to be rid of.

In addition, however, Martha was probably thrusting away an implication more unkind and a disability less temporary. At the time of the Roman sojourn she was 29 or 30. She must have felt in danger of passing the rest of her life as a spinster of whom domesticated favours and chores could be demanded by everyone in the large household of Smarmore Castle. She might indeed want to repudiate the associations that had attended the name she bore ever since the gospel of Saint Luke hung domesticity about the neck of a Martha – and a Martha, moreover, who had a sister more interesting than herself.

It was standing side by side that Gagarin drew the sisters (on drawing paper watermarked 1826). His picture was done in May 1832, which was probably near the end of their visit to Rome, but he shews them as they must have looked at a score of balls and parties both before and after Lent.

Draping a curtain behind them, the hanging, perhaps, of an embrasure where they intend to refresh themselves between sets of dances, Gagarin hints a parody of a grand double portrait. Indeed, Julia holds her furled fan much as a field marshall might hold his jewelled baton.

At the same time, the girls are framed like goods in a shop window – which, crudely, they were. Martha-Joanna was already in danger of the crude metaphor of being left on the shelf, victim of the cruel system operated by the classes whose distinguishing adjective for themselves was 'gentle'.

Martha-Joanna stands a little taller than her sister – as though, by unkind accident, she is still, even now they are both adult, bodily marked out as the elder.

That implication is no doubt what Martha-Joanna is discountenancing by dressing identically, down to their very jewellery, with her junior. In all the pictures by Gagarin where Martha-Joanna appears, she and Julia are dressed alike. Martha was visually twinning herself with Julia. And when, having discarded the name Martha, she picked on Joanna to replace it, she was twinning herself audibly and in initials with Julia as well.

Martha-Joanna is a little too tall, perhaps, to be in great demand among dancing partners. She is already touched by a slight stateliness that, like her headdress and built-up hair, could easily topple into caricature. Perhaps for fear of toppling her headdress, she evidently finds it quite acceptable to keep still, and she gazes, with a mild expression of nothing much, at nothing much – or perhaps at her future.

Julia has been caught a little flat footed by her portraitist's demand that she freeze while her likeness is taken. Turning, she seems impatient to turn back and resume her animation. Hers is the liveliness and, if Gagarin's implications are correct, the flirtatiousness and the caprice of the petted youngest of a large family. Constrained to keep briefly still, she tilts her head and stares directly at Gagarin, by no means without expression but with a meaning too ambivalent to read.

---

6   *Paddies on a Terrace*

She is far from the land where her young hero sleeps
And lovers are round her, sighing:
But coldly she turns from their gaze, and weeps,
For her heart in his grave is lying.

She sings the wild songs of her dear native plains . . .

IT IS PROBABLE that, so soon as she declared herself Irish, Julia was pressed by her hosts and her fellow-guests at the Villa Medici to sing them the wild songs of Ireland.

No doubt she was accompanied, at Louise Vernet's pianoforte, by Martha-Joanna, whose destiny it seems to have been to accompany Julia.

Julia's dear native plains had not taken so early or so strong a hold as Scotland on the imagination of Europe. Romantics seeking wildness found chiefly confusion in a history where betrayal was as compulsive and repetitive as rebellion and a land where so many heroes slept that it was difficult to distinguish one grave from another.

The young hero of Thomas Moore's lament is in fact Robert Emmet, betrayed and hanged, at the age of 25, in 1803. The she who is far from Ireland is his sweetheart, Sarah Curran, who, after the execution of Emmet, married an English army officer and went with him, when the British garrison there was reinforced, to Sicily.

For impressing its individuality on Europe, Ireland, though it had the kilt, lacked a fabric as fauve and distinctive as plaid in which to carry it out. It also lacked a Mary, Queen of Scots. The Shan Van Voght, the poor old woman who personified Ireland, was not up to the bravura of the rôle. The political history of the 19th century would have taken a different turn had it been a Mary, Queen of the Irish whom Schiller and Donizetti, on their various occasions, made into an international heroine – or indeed had Walter Scott and Donizetti created a Lucia di Limerick.

The Shan Van Voght might insist as often as she would that the French were on the sea, sailing to the liberation of Ireland, but Ireland in fact lacked an Auld Alliance, as it did an Ossian and a Scott.

It had, however, Tom Moore.

As Julia's lovers, sighing for love, crowded about the piano, Prince Grégoire Gagarin may well have conceived a hatred for the wild songs that Thomas Moore and the musician Sir John Stevenson had apparently tamed to the drawing room but had left with an irrefragable power to bring a lump to the throat. As Julia coldly or at least ambivalently turned from his gaze, he must have feared that she was turning also from the exile of the wild geese.

If the audience included Hector Berlioz, he will surely have taken the song as his cue to recount how he had, at his fifth attempt, won his Prix de Rome, writing the closing bars of his competition cantata at the very moment when the small revolution of July 1830 broke out in Paris. He left the examination room to spend the few days that the revolution took wandering Paris with a pistol in his hand and exaltation in his heart. Passing through the Palais Royal, he heard men singing a tune he recognised. It was of his own composing. The words he had set were from Thomas Moore's *Irish Melodies:*

> Forget not our wounded companions, who stood
>   In the day of distress by our side;
> While the moss of the valley grew red with their blood
>   They stirred not, but conquered and died.

To this Julia will certainly have rejoined that Thomas Moore's latest (1831) publication was *The Life and Death of Lord Edward FitzGerald* and that she and her sister were in Rome under the quasi-parental care of Lord Edward's nephew.

That seems the implication of Gagarin's picture of the whole party on a terrace on the Monte Pincio as interpreted by Julia's great-niece's identifying note.

Lord Edward FitzGerald was a hero appropriate to Berlioz's song. He indeed died (in 1798) of his wounds, which were received, however, not in battle, because he was betrayed by a fellow-conspirator before his rebellion was raised, but during his arrest.

(Thackeray, whose unrealised presence shadows the story of Julia Taaffe and Grégoire Gagarin, read Moore's *Life* in the autumn of 1831 and reported to his friend, the Edward FitzGerald who later wrote or translated *The Rubaiyat of Omar Khayyám*, namesake of Moore's subject: 'The reason I liked & like Ld Edward FitzGerald so much was from his likeness to you.')

The FitzGeralds were among the grandest of Anglo-Irish grandees, Earls of Kildare and, from the 18th century, Dukes of Leinster. They were Whigs and, for the most part, of liberal inclination, opponents of the Act of Union forced through by the younger Pitt to the destruction of even the appearance of Irish autonomy. Lord Edward, a son of the first Duke of Leinster, had been Rousseauist, deist, egalitarian, revolutionary and patriot. After his death, his sister, Lady Lucy, in a manifesto that began 'Irishmen, Countrymen', declared herself willing to die for Ireland as her brother had done and continued: 'I don't mean to remind you of what he did for you. 'Twas no more than his duty . . . He was *a Paddy and no more*; he desired no other title than this.'

His nephew, Lord William Charles O'Brien FitzGerald, second of the two sons of the second Duke, was, in the spring of 1832, 39. Gagarin catches a certain long, Irish horsiness about his face but makes him a fashionable and rather commanding figure (who may, indeed, be about to warn off the admirer leaning over the railings to gaze down on Julia), as you might expect of someone whose brother, now the third Duke of Leinster, was a godson of the Prince Regent and who had himself proved unflinching under fire when, a second-year undergraduate at Oxford, he spent the long vacation of 1811 at Wellington's headquarters in Spain.

In her note to another picture, Julia's great-niece describes Lord William FitzGerald as Julia's step-father. That he certainly was not. Neither is the problem solved by the obvious conjecture that 'step-father' was a slip of the pen for 'godfather'. At the time of Julia's baptism Lord William was a schoolboy – and, moreover, a Protestant schoolboy. The probability is that 'step-father' was used, certainly by the note-writer and quite possibly by Julia herself, to indicate a remote family connexion too tedious to explain with exactitude plus a strong degree of responsibility taken on by Lord William towards the orphaned and as yet unmarried Taaffe girls.

To bring them into the FitzGerald sphere of influence was probably what John Taaffe *fils* had achieved for his sisters by his own first marriage, which was to a daughter of General Andrew FitzGerald, who had served with the British Army in India.

Thus, probably, it came about that in 1832 Julia and Martha-Joanna were enjoying the Roman spring, on a terrace cut into the declivity of the Pincian Hill, under the protection of Lord William FitzGerald and the chaperonage of Lady William.

The FitzGeralds are presumably the parents of the two children (of whom the girl is claimed by Julia's great-niece as her grandmother) and the owners of the corgi-like but Spitz-tailed dog.

The temperature has advanced further into spring than the foliage. Even so, the women are well muffled (Lady William FitzGerald, the nearest of them, in something that looks like an Italian parody of tartan), though the sun is strong enough for Lady William and Martha-Joanna to have put up their parasols.

Perhaps the charm of the weather has inclined Julia's heart towards Gagarin. Evidently he is accepted by the FitzGeralds, if not by Julia herself, as a quasi-official suitor for her hand (and who more eligible?), since he has been allowed to appoint himself quasi-official portraitist to this group of posh Paddies on a terrace.

Yet Gagarin's eye is still jealously alert to rivals. Lord William seems not to have spotted, though his little boy has, the heavily moustached man who will even lean on a hedge to get a closer view of Julia. And another, with an oval face of slightly insipid sweetness, has actually insinuated himself into the group, accepted certainly as an acquaintance and perhaps as a suitor, since he is sitting next to Julia and one of his hands, in their lemon yellow gloves, rests in a most accepted way on her unopened parasol.

Both men were to recur in Gagarin's drawings.

---

7 *A Sentimental View*

THE HAND that wrote the title on the drawing is not Gagarin's. He would in any case have written in French. Neither is it the hand of Julia's great-niece, who in any case wrote her notes not on the pictures or in the album but on detached pieces of paper. It must be Julia herself who inscribed: 'A View on the Pincian.'

a View on the
Pincian —

But the joke is Gagarin's.

No doubt Julia had asked him to draw something 'nice' (a concept she no doubt rendered as 'joli') for a change.

He complied by offering that 'nicest' of subjects, beloved of amateur draughtsmen and sighed over by amateur connoisseurs, a view.

When he put away his pencil and handed her the drawing, it turned out that he had delineated not vegetable life but animal and had satirised not the subject but the person who requested the drawing.

The view Julia is really seeking, Gagarin implies, as she so regularly takes the air on the Pincian, is of the sweet, oval, insipid face of the admirer who had sat next to her on the terrace.

8 Masquerade

OF A SUDDEN, all the small, cave-like shops of Rome were offering the same wares – masks.

From stalls at street corners hawkers cried sweetmeats: destined not for eating but for throwing.

The eternal city became hectic and headlong – and raucous. Scaffolding was banged into place and platforms balanced across it. Posters spurted on house walls to announce the times of the horse races. Tar barrels were manhandled into lines along the gutters and lit when the precipitate southern dusk descended. Flaming torches outlined roofs and pediments. By night, the dome of Saint Peter's blazed in an empurpled sky. Fireworks exploded and dropped their fiery flowers into the Tiber.

Rome was in Carnival, the feast of farewell to feasting.

Anonymous behind masks bizarre, whimsical or grotesque, everyone accosted everyone in the packed streets. Well-bred girls, even well-bred English girls, leaned from balconies and pelted men driving in open carriages below with sweetmeats or flowers, according to their judgment on the attractiveness of the target. Everyone who could afford to own or hire a carriage drove several times a day up and down the Corso, while the carriage filled up with sweet booty. Men on foot clutched bouquets thrust on them by giggling girls – or, rather, if you went by their seeming faces, by giggling wild animals, monsters, devils, nymphs, Muses . . .

The French and the Spanish embassies gave their customary grand balls.

At the Villa Medici, the entertainment was more intimate, though scarcely less crowded, and more fanciful: something, it appears, between a masquerade and a charade.

A court of fantastic beings receives the commands of a monarch who, enthroned, crowned, long-bearded and apparently long-eared, resembles a sea-king. Perhaps the rôle was designed for and played by the friend whom Hector Berlioz described as 'Munier, the marine painter' and whom the students nick-named, because of his subject-matter, Neptune. (If he is the Émile Munier who was born in 1810 and was still exhibiting at the Salon in Paris in 1895, he broadened his subject-matter later in his career.) One of the women who form the half participating audience at the left of the picture has doffed her mask (the clue that identifies the picture as a Carnival scene). Perhaps she guesses that Gagarin will extract enough grotesquerie from the fashion for squat, off-the-shoulder dresses with bouncy sleeves and the high, tripartite coiffures that make a woman's head, seen from the back, look like the head and ears of a rather scrawnily furred animal.

The fruit-tree in the background of the court episode is at the centre of the sequel. Perhaps it is a real tree shifted bodily indoors, though, given the time of year, its fruits must be counterfeit, or perhaps it bears witness to the craftsmanship of the Villa Medici students of painting and sculpture.

What is being acted out is clearly a drama, spoken or mimed, but its plot is no longer to be followed and its *dramatis personae* are now baffling. A woman in 18th-century dress receives a whispered message from a sort of bear in the tree, while the hero or villain, whose costume seems tinged with the oriental, subjugates the small creature with a long tail who, in the court episode, squatted in front of the monarch's dais.

The actor who plays the creature with the long tail is no doubt a child. At least, he has real toys, which have got into the entertainment or at any rate into Gagarin's picture of it.

And somehow Gagarin's own imagination has made the whole occasion look more than a little Russian, not so much masquerade as ballet, almost an anticipation of *The Nutcracker*.

9 Triumph

ON SHROVE TUESDAY, which in 1832 fell on the 6th of March, Rome roared at the summit of the Carnival crescendo; and Grégoire Gagarin's imagination soared in hyperbole.

The Carnival processions, far from diverting his thoughts, concentrated them on Julia Taaffe.

He conceived Julia's triumph – a triumph of the kind that ancient Rome accorded its generals when they returned victorious from major campaigns against foreign enemies. The homecoming victor was conducted from the outskirts of the city (or in Gagarin's version from the coast at Naples, whither favouring winds, as in old maps, have wafted the ship) to the Capitol, in a triumphal car, accompanied by the magistrates (the government) and the Senate, followed by his soldiers and preceded by the captives he had taken during the campaign.

Julia in Rome was such a victor. She came, she was seen, she conquered.

Her predecessor, Julius Caesar, the feminine form of whose name she bore (which was probably the ignition point for Gagarin's flight of fantasy), had been able to make captive only his contemporaries, though he managed also to captivate historians who came after and to imprison generations of schoolboys who were forced to construe his *Gallic Wars*.

Julia's captives of course include contemporaries. They constitute the middle tier of her wedding-cake-like triumphal car, where they perform the function of caryatides in classical architecture, though, being flesh and blood, they are of uneven height and one is so short that he has to stand both on a cushion and on tiptoe to reach the required uniform level. Enthroned, Julia is borne up by the shoulders of her suitors, including the burly shoulders of the Thackerayesque man who was one of her victims when she played Cupid and the slightly shrinking, stooped shoulders of his fellow-wearer of spectacles.

Gagarin's imagination, however, refuses to admit any limitations of time on Julia's supremacy. 'The centuries', says the title of his picture in French, 'pay homage to the perfect woman' (and Julia's great-niece, translating it in her note, fails to observe that *homage*, which has two *m*'s in French, has only one in English).

In Julia Taaffe's triumphal procession, Julius Caesar himself (at the left of the front rank as the throng advances) is captive to Julia; and his bald, wreathed brow jostles crowned heads, mitred heads, the biretta'd head of Richelieu, the tricorned head of Frederick the Great, a turban (Saladin's, perhaps) and the feathered head of, presumably, Montezuma.

The centre of the front rank reads, resplendently, from left to right: Moses (Gagarin had occupied some of his time in Rome in looking at Michelangelo's statue of him in San Pietro in Vincoli), Louis XIV, a pharaoh, François Premier. A Chinese sage or warlord presses forward from the rank behind.

Julia has conquered the conquerors, the captains, kings and knights – and not only those who had a factual existence. Between Frederick (who is near the extreme right, beside a putative Alexander or Mark Antony) and what appears to be a patriarch of the Russian church marches Don Quixote.

Yet again, and perhaps with reason, Gagarin has cast Julia as a belligerent.

Her success in Roman society, her sack of Rome, is enlarged into a conquest of the world, and it is a world without distinctions of time. All history, Gagarin declares, is merely a jumbled procession that culminates in Julia.

10 'Fi Donc, Monsieur Grégoire'

ONCE LENT had descended, Grégoire Gagarin could no longer count on meeting Julia at some party or other virtually every evening. No doubt he formed instead the habit of calling daily at the house or set of rooms that the FitzGerald-Taaffe group had rented in the Via del Babuino, which runs into the Piazza di Spagna.

There, it is to be supposed, he called one morning and found the group gone.

Quickly he was reassured – most likely by the servants. The FitzGeralds and the Taaffe girls had departed only on a tour, taking advantage of the Lenten lull in social affairs to travel and sight-see.

In two carriages, with a waggon for their luggage in between, they had set off down the Via Appia, the ancient road from Rome to Capua that had begun building, while Appius Claudius Caecus held the office of censor, in 312 BC, their first stop Albano in the Alban Hills and their ultimate destination Naples – a journey for which in 1832 AD travellers from Rome had to equip themselves with passports, since Naples was the capital of the autonomous Kingdom of the Two Sicilies.

The group was surely expected back in Rome in good time for Easter, whose date in 1832 was the 22nd of April, since they would not want to miss the musically and visually spectacular ceremonies to be conducted by the Pope (Gregory XVI, who had been elected the previous year) on Palm Sunday and during Holy Week.

Something, however, of Gagarin's first shock when he found Julia gone remains in the letter he sent after her to Naples.

He felt reduced. In keeping, the vignettes that decorate his letter are miniature (and more than ever Thackerayesque).

At the top, by way of letterhead, he drew a miniature scene he entitled 'The devil's magic lantern'.

The audience at this magic lantern show wears 16th- and 17th-century dress, with the exception of two women in clothes of the 1830s, who,

LA LANTERNE MAGIQUE DU DIABLE

Ce petit animal qui ressemble à un homme c'est le soussigné, les yeux fixés sur le creux d'une ornière de la route d'Albano. Pourquoi cette ornière attire-t-elle l'attention de cet individu plus que tout autre sillon tracé dans la poussière ou la boue? Écoutez ce qu'il répond: (il a parfois des inspirations classiques) Quand pourrai-je au travers d'une noble poussière

  Suivre de l'œil un char fuyant dans la carrière!

  mais un char qui ne serait pas un char... mais qui serait ce donc? un tilbury, un cabriolet, ou un phaéton ou non — un.... point du tout, voyez plutôt c'est une berline Anglaise. Eh bon voyage! comme ses rapides chevaux l'entraînent!

though one can't be sure because their backs are turned, are probably the Taaffe sisters. Gagarin is reminding Julia of the Carnival entertainment at the Villa Medici and perhaps of a costume ball there. He probably hopes to remind her of his own portrait, drawn at the Villa Medici by Horace Vernet, as a 16th-century hero.

Gagarin was uncertain how Julia, given that she had not cared to forewarn him of her departure, would respond to receiving a letter from him. Neither could he be sure that Martha-Joanna or even Lady William FitzGerald would not insist on reading the letter too. He disarms reproach by signalling at the top that it is to be a nonsense letter, a children's entertainment.

The quasi-letterhead dispenses his letter from beginning with a formal salutation – which, were it too formal, would excite jeers from Julia but, were it not formal enough and were it to be seen by chaperoning eyes, would risk compromising her.

Beside a miniature portrait of himself pacing the Appian Way, whose ancient milestones are still *in situ* (along with the ancient tombs and catacombs beside it that made it required visiting for tourists), he opens directly, in his practised French and his legible, schoolroom hand – whose neat law-abidingness, with its long *s*'s for the first component of a double *s*, betokens not only the manual control of a draughtsman but the fact that the western alphabet was the second alphabet he mastered.

Under the mantle of fiction he declares that, by leaving him to deduce where she has gone from such clues as he can find, Julia has shrunken him.

'This little animal who looks like a man is the undersigned, his eyes bent on the hollow of a rut on the road to Albano. Why does this rut attract this individual's attention beyond all other furrows traced in the dust or the mud?

'Listen', he continues in children's story-book manner, 'to his answer.'

The answer, however, is couched in terms of the adult aesthetic debate that Stendhal had set in train between Classicism and Romanticism.

'Sometimes', Gagarin remarks in brackets, 'he' (still the 'petit animal') 'has classical inspirations.' And he goes on to quote

> Quand pourrai-je, au travers d'une noble poussière,
> Suivre de l'oeil un char fuyant dans la carrière?

– the almost visionary question, 'When shall I be able, through a noble dust, to follow by eye a chariot fleeing in its course?', that forces itself from the distraught lips of Racine's Phèdre during the scene where she makes her first appearance in the play.

This 'classical inspiration' he illustrates with a vignette of an ancient-world chariot and charioteer, whose own inspiration is not so much Euripides by way of Racine as, surely, Bryulov's painting of the last days of Pompeii.

Already, however, Gagarin's magic lantern is changing the image. 'But a chariot,' his letter goes on, 'that isn't a chariot . . . but what is it then? a tilbury, a cabriolet, or a phaeton or not – a . . . not at all – Look, it is, rather, an English berlin. Well bon voyage! How', he exclaims, again in the cadence of a picture book or magic lantern show for children, 'its swift horses are dragging it along!'

And in the next vignette the chariot has been transformed (and its direction across the page reversed) into a modern carriage, with Lady William FitzGerald inside and the Taaffe girls perched, uncomfortably but dashingly, outside.

However, the swift carriage, Gagarin continues on his second page, fictionalising his feeling of loss and his fears for the future, is quickly 'no more than a dot that sinks into the vapour of the atmosphere, it mingles with the blue of the mountains, it has vanished like a young man's dream, it is lost like a beautiful plan for the future . . . What is he to do? What will become of him? Hang himself.'

There follows a row of vignettes of desperate deeds. He hangs from a gallows. He launches himself from a bridge into a torrent. He presses himself to the mouth of a cannon and tries to ignite the charge himself. He tries to operate himself the lever that will make the blade of a guillotine descend on him. He shoots himself. He defenestrates himself.

The reproach his text then addresses to himself is in the tones of Julia, the Julia who, deploring the bloodshed attributed to her as Cupid, asked him for a 'nice' or 'joli' picture – of, for instance, that irreproachable subject, a view on the Pincian.

'Fi donc, Monsieur Grégoire – Fie, Monsieur Grégoire, you always draw extremely ugly things, how can one take pleasure in gibbets and guillotines, don't think of it . . .'

He replies, in a dialogue that is imaginary but whose substance had certainly passed between them many times:

'Alas, it's for want of better!'

'How is it that you don't know how to depict more graceful subjects?'

'I'd be only too glad to, but for that it's necessary to go some distance, since here everything is fatal, black and sinister.'

At this point, having declared his desolation, Gagarin takes off into the comfortingness (for himself) and the entertainment (for, he hopes, Julia) of fantasy.

A vignette mounts him on a magic horse. Naming the towns he knows or guesses, from having made the journey himself, to be the stopping-places on Julia's itinerary, 'I leap in two bounds', says his text, 'over Terracina, Mola di Gaeta, Capua, I stop for some time at Aversa, where there is a lunatic asylum . . .'

Wherever possible, he gives the place-names their French form – Terracine, the regular half-way point on the Rome-Naples route, and Capoue. But there is no gallicising Mola di Gaeta (which is not Gaeta itself but its neighbour along the coast-line, a town that later, after the reunification of Italy, took the name Formia, a resumption of its ancient name of Formiae) or Aversa (which is a little north of and inland from Naples).

The word *temps* Gargarin spells, correctly at the period but perhaps already a little old-fashionedly, without its *p*.

'And from there', his narrative continues, 'I launch myself upon the watery plain, I swim in the huge blue Ocean, Naples' (whose bay forms a vignette) 'defines itself in front of me like a splendid amphitheatre, in which the chief box, the one that strikes my gaze, is the hotel de la *victoire*.'

(The Vittoria was the first of the hotels at Naples mentioned by an English guide book of 1828; and in 1896 Baedeker was still giving it one of the asterisks 'used as marks of commendation'. It was in the Via Partenope, which adjoins the Largo della Vittoria and fronts onto the bay.)

What is so striking about the Vittoria hotel is disclosed on Gagarin's third page, which begins, mock-heroically:

'It is to reach there that so many noble hearts have thrilled in men's broad breasts, that famed heroes . . . heaven! what do I see! the English berlin is arriving, it stops here, then a wagon, then another berlin. God! it is they, it is she! I forget that I am swimming, my powers fail me, I sink, I am with monstrous sharks in the black, cold caverns that are at the bottom of the watery domain.'

He depicts himself, a naked, vulnerable white outline in the black, cold cavern, circled by a pair of (presumably) sharks with a certain resemblance to goldfish.

Taking the opportunity to mock Julia's demands for 'joli' subject-matter, he breaks off to comment in the tones of a nanny removing her charge from an unsuitable magic lantern show 'But this has much the air of a high fever' and to issue the warning, as though for an audience young and easily scared indeed, 'the story we are telling you here is not at all joli'.

The story, which has not only the summary movement of a story for (or even by) children but a little of the surreal waywardness that baffles and charms foreigners in translations of long, semi-narrative Russian proverbs, resumes with an 'Excuse me' in dialogue.

'A crocodile', the narrator explains, 'is introducing himself at my right. Even as I flee from his murderous gullet, a shark with a triple row of teeth cuts off my retreat at my left.'

Perhaps the circling monsters who beset Gagarin are his rivals in love, who encircled Julia on the dance floor and who import danger to him as well as pressure on her.

Fairy tales, however, can have quick and happy endings. 'In this cruel dilemma', the story goes on, 'guess what happened. The crocodile devoured the shark and while they set about one another I give them the slip, I return to the surface, the day is serene, the sky is pure. I see Vesuvius with its mouth smoking, again I see the temple of victory.'

The coast-line of Naples, so rich in ancient temples, has acquired a new one, in honour of the hotel that is housing Julia.

And if the hotel is Victory, the guests who stay at it are victors. 'J'apperçois mes vainqueurs', the story continues, ' – I catch sight of my conquerors in a light boat ploughing across the bay of Pozzuoli.'

The victors who have made a conquest of Gagarin are, of course, the FitzGerald-Taaffe party, and what Gagarin sees them doing, in the first three vignettes on his final page, is following the regular tourist routine of Naples.

He sees them on the bay of Pozzuoli (which he renders in French as Puzzoles), with other tourists, in a boat that has both sail and oars.

'I see them on the coppery back of a strong lazzarone as they go to ask their fortune in the sombre grotto of an illustrious sibyl.' Perhaps they are visiting the supposed grotto of the Cumaean Sibyl on the outskirts of

Naples or perhaps they are being carried into the Blue Grotto on Capri, whose entrance rises only a few feet above the surface of the sea and which had become popular since its rediscovery in 1826.

'I see them on the back of this animal' (he draws one of the donkeys who were hired out to tourists at Naples for mountainous sight-seeing trips) 'who' (in an allusion to the behaviour of Balaam's ass in *Numbers*) 'alone among animals knew how to get his tongue round the language of humans.' And to complete the Old Testament reference, it is a line of mock-Hebrew characters that issues from the donkey's braying mouth.

Gagarin is about to go on to picture the party at the most celebrated of Neapolitan tourist sites but he deliberately breaks off.

'I see them on Vesu . . . I see them, that is to say I do not see them.'

He draws himself sitting up suddenly, staring-eyed, at his table, with its reading light, in Rome.

'It was a joli dream. I wake up hobbledehoy as before, lodging on the Piazza Navona, with which I have the honour to be what one is at the end of a letter' (he avoids committing himself to the correct degree of formality for his ending as for his beginning) 'and, furthermore, the most devoted of your 100,000 servants.'

And with a final self-portrait in the shape of the quite undiabolic presenter of the magic lantern show taking his bow at the end, the promised 'undersigned' signs himself, with a calligraphic flourish to match his bow, 'Me'.

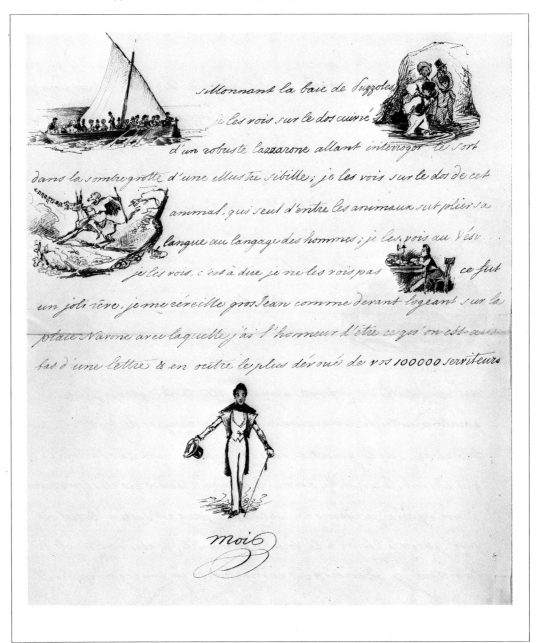

sillonnant la baie de Puzzoles,

je les vois sur le dos cuivré

d'un robuste lazzarone allant interroger le sort

dans la sombre grotte d'une illustre sibille; je les vois sur le dos de cet

animal, qui seul d'entre les animaux sut plier sa

langue au langage des hommes; je les vois au Vésu...

je les vois, c'est à dire je ne les vois pas   ce fut

un joli rêve, je me réveille gros Jean comme devant logeant sur la

place Navone avec laquelle j'ai l'honneur d'être ce que'on est au

bas d'une lettre & en outre le plus dévoué de vos 100000 serviteurs

moi

11 Balcony Scene at the Vittoria

OF THE MANY letters Gagarin must have written her, the illustrated one, which he sent after her to Naples when he discovered she could be addressed there at the hotel Vittoria (and which consists of a large sheet folded in two to create four pages) was the only one Julia Taaffe kept.

She prized his drawings. Did she set smaller store by his words and sentiments?

Perhaps she intended to use her absence from him during her stay in Naples as an opportunity to search her feelings and find out.

Left behind in Rome, Grégoire Gagarin was prey to spleen and jealousy and, presently, rumour.

Perhaps the sight of Gagarin, haunting like a spectre what now seemed to him an empty Rome, impressed itself on the circle where he was usually noted for his liveliness. Perhaps the disconsolate image of the young Russian whose acquaintance he had made in an English-speaking group at the Villa Medici lodged in the imagination of Hector Berlioz and led him, some two months later when he suffered an access of spleen himself, to describe his sense of being alienated with the words 'I seem to be not myself but some stranger – some Russian or Englishman'.

Whether Gagarin heard from Julia while she was in Naples is unknown. Certainly, however, he heard of her, no doubt in the gossip of a returned traveller.

The note Julia's great-niece wrote to Gagarin's picture of the incident is circumstantial and clearly correct; the story must have planted itself with particular firmness in her memory when she heard it from Julia in her childhood. 'An admirer of our Great aunt Julia bringing up a glove she had dropped – in Naples now – Prince Grègoire (*sic*) Gagarin had heard of the incident – & sent her this drawing of it.'

In Gagarin's picture, the hotel Vittoria indeed, as Baedeker was later to promise, looks over the sea, which has a sailing boat on it. Julia, enjoying the sea breeze on a balcony, dangles over the railings the gloves which the proprieties bade her carry but the spring warmth forbids her to wear, and has let one fall.

The admirer who has retrieved it, brought it upstairs and restored it to her is given, by Gagarin, whether through knowledge or through suspicion, the face and the indeed hedge-textured moustache of the man who gazed over a hedge at Julia on the Pincian.

As he hands back her white one, he is himself wearing lemon yellow gloves, like those worn on the Pincian by his sweet and oval faced rival. Perhaps they were in fashion that spring. Or perhaps word had been passed among Julia's admirers that she liked them.

Gagarin clearly suspects the hedge-moustached man of having followed Julia to Naples in the hope of just such an opportunity to do her a service. Indeed, he probably suspects Julia of having dropped her glove on purpose.

At Rome, Berlioz perhaps cited the works of Shakespeare to warn his Russian acquaintance against allowing suspicion to pin jealousy to such bits of fabric as gloves and handkerchiefs.

Never the less, Gagarin sent the drawing to Julia at Naples.

And she, debating with herself what her feelings towards Gagarin might be, probably took warning from the fierceness of his warning to her.

12 A Non-Duel

As often happens to people who withdraw for an interval in which to make up their minds, Julia returned to Rome with her feelings towards Grégoire Gagarin unresolved.

Social gatherings resumed after the 22nd of April. As they gained force and pace, so did the pressure on Julia to choose a husband. In May she was well enough disposed to Gagarin to pause during a ball and let him make his double portrait of herself and Martha-Joanna, even though standing still made her impatient.

Impatience was perhaps her chief response: both to the rather humiliating insistence of her family circle that she must marry someone and to the more flattering and provocative, if less easily fobbed off, insistence of each suitor that she should marry, precisely and uniquely, *him*.

And it was probably in good part her impatience, whether you read it as the ungovernability of a youngest child or the wildness of an Irish rebel, that drew suitors to her in such numbers.

Gagarin, of course, exaggerated their numbers. He was himself so many fathoms deep in love with Julia, over his head and deep in black, cold caverns in love with her, that it seemed to him not merely natural but inevitable that everyone else should be too.

It was no more than logical of him to spy an admirer behind every hedge. Had none been there, he would have accused the hedge of flirting with Julia and Julia of responding.

Admirers, however, truly were there: fewer than the 100,000 cast up by Gagarin's hyperbolic and jealous fantasy but quite enough to cause Julia bewilderment – and also, no doubt, surprise.

After all, she was not beautiful.

Still, she possessed in Rome what she never could in Ireland: exoticism. She arrived at a moment when tribal culture was at the height of fashion, even though hers was not the most fashionable tribe.

Perversely, the piquant value which her Irishness took on in Rome

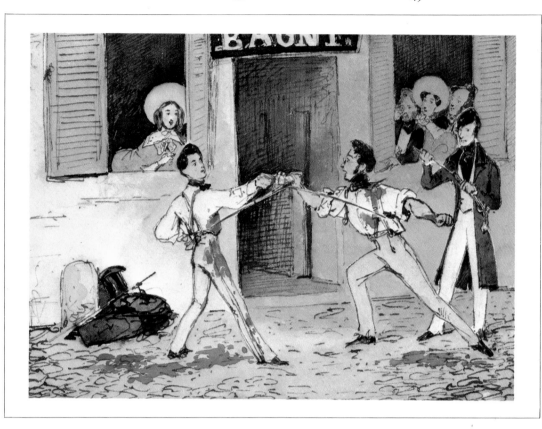

probably worked to close her impatient heart against the wild-geese
solution of taking, in Rome, a foreign husband.

Yet Irishness alone was not (witness Martha-Joanna, who was every bit
as Irish as Julia) enough to make a triumph.

Julia's particular type of non-beauty was even more fashionable than
tribalism – more fashionable, indeed, than beauty.

Irish society was no doubt some way behind the fashion, and in Ireland
not only the knowing and match-making chaperones lining the ballrooms
but also young men with hearts to pledge were still scrutinising young
women's faces to discern the Grecian accents of classical beauty.

It must, therefore, have astonished and, at first, exhilarated Julia to
discover, on reaching Rome, that her type of looks was much more up-to-
date.

You could read into her face at least a capacity for tenderness; and at the same time it was a face that openly shewed a quickness to be amused or bored. It would be easy to pass off Gagarin's portrait of Julia and her sister as a picture of the heroine (perhaps noble, perhaps peasant, perhaps the one disguised as the other) of a lost Donizetti opera, with her (no doubt mezzo-soprano) *confidente*.

If the exhilaration which that discovery caused Julia turned into impatience, as things inclined to do quite quickly with Julia, it was no doubt because, in the exercise of her surprising success, she made another discovery – and one that, above all, she could not, in tact and decency, confide to Martha-Joanna. Collecting men's hearts like trophies or wild flowers was, of all forms of collecting, the least profitable in terms of pleasure. The love of a man you did not love was non-convertible currency. You could not change it into even a small quantity of the love of a man, if one existed, whom you did love. You could not swop it, as you could other unwanted collector's items, with a collector who had a place or a need for it. You could not make it over, like a piece of jewellery or a pair of gloves, to a Martha-Joanna whose own wardrobe was deficient.

When Julia reproached Gagarin for always drawing 'de bien vilaines choses' and asked what pleasure could be taken in such subject-matter, she might have gone on to ask what pleasure was to be had from possessing the utter and abject devotion of a man to whom one was not devoted oneself.

What provoked Julia's impatience with Gagarin was probably not the scrape he now got himself into, which she was high-spirited enough to get both him and herself out of with ease, but the obtusity with which, seeing lovers of Julia everywhere, he assumed that their attentions enriched Julia, though in reality she could not spend the coin.

Likewise he seemed to assume that, if he could cut down his rivals, that would increase the likelihood of Julia's giving her heart to him.

All the same, the one thing that is clear about the duel Gagarin depicted between himself and the spectacled admirer of Julia who appears both among the victims of Julia-Cupid and among the caryatides of her triumphal car is that the incident it reflects was not a duel.

Duels were not fought on the city cobbles among shops and commercial establishments even of a dubious kind.

Besides, Gagarin signals his comic intention by picturing the duellists in their shirt sleeves, thereby putting on display their braces, those unheroic concomitants of unheroic modern trousers.

Perhaps there was some horseplay, with foils borrowed from the students at the Villa Medici, who were given to athletic pursuits. Or perhaps Gagarin is simply fictionalising an altercation.

The altercation or whatever it was must have taken place publicly enough to cause scandal. Gagarin implies that their wounds are public knowledge by covering both duellists with blood – no doubt provoking Julia to complain that he was again depicting 'de bien vilaines choses'. Besides, there are witnesses. Gagarin's opponent has a second; and the duel is watched by Martha-Joanna, with two companions, at one window and, at the other, Julia herself.

Julia's great-niece took the duel seriously, perhaps with the seriousness of the child she was when Julia led her through Gagarin's pictures as his letter had led Julia herself through his magic lantern show. Her note remarks that Julia is watching the duel and says that Gagarin is fighting it 'on her behalf.'

Did he suppose, then, that the prize, in even a fictitious duel, was Julia's hand? He knew well that that was not the way to win it. He was, after all, the son of a diplomatist and he had shewn himself skilled at wooing Julia with pictures and a nonsense entertainment.

Then does 'on her behalf' imply that he was fighting to vindicate Julia's honour? But would an admirer slavish enough to serve as a caryatid ever have impugned it?

And what does Gagarin's own picture (or the circumstances of the real incident of which that is a dramatised version) say of Julia's honour?

What is she doing at the window of this in both senses low establishment, with the notice 'Baths' over its evil door, which in another social context one might suspect of being a brothel?

And why, if it is not true (*is* it true?), does Gagarin, who early implied that Julia took a callous pleasure in wounding men's hearts herself, now imply that she has progressed to a more sophisticated delight in setting men on to wound one another?

13   A Frozen Dialogue

There were now frequent social gatherings where Gagarin could meet Julia. But they availed him nothing.

She became cold to him.

Was she angered by the non-duel? Or by the rôle Gagarin's picture of it ascribed to her?

Freezing his polished politenesses, his social ease and his flirtatiousness on his lips, she receives his attentions not with mere impatience, though she sits well forward and thus gestures her wish to be up, out of her deep armchair and off to some more entertaining part of the room, but with conspicuous, all but back-turning indifference.

'Madam, I am your servant . . .'

'I detest people who are importunate.'

'Does your health continue good?'

'In what way are you involved? It's no concern of yours.'

Gagarin was angered in turn.

Unsure how seriously to take his own anger, because he cannot tell how serious or lasting hers is, he satirises himself, giving his picture of their frozen conversation three titles or headlines, two mock-heroic and the third mock-splenetic, each in larger letters than the one above:

A SET PURPOSE
HEROIC RESOLUTION
HATRED FOR WOMEN!

But his mock-melodramatics are given the lie, he hopes, by the intimacy that still exists between Julia and him. He labels the lines of their dialogue with the initials of their first names only.

Likewise, the 'heroic resolution' he tries to draw in his face is belied by the accommodating, peace-making inclination of his figure towards hers.

And indeed his sending her the drawing was an act of peace.

Un parti pris.
Résolution héroïque
Haine aux femmes!

Amabilités Irlandaises

G.ᵈ *Mad.ᵉ je suis bien votre serviteur* . . . .

J. *Je déteste les importuns*

G. *Votre santé, est elle toujours bonne?*

J. *De quoi vous mêlez vous, ça ne vous regarde pas.*

Yet if he reads hope in the fact that her coldness (like his hatred of women) was clearly, if not assumed, dramatised in order to make a point, he is afraid that it is genuine too.

He suspects that Julia has discovered that she cannot bring herself to quit Ireland and become a wild goose.

It is Ireland he blames for her turning away from him. The title he gives the frozen dialogue is 'Irish Amiabilities'.

14 An Expedition

GAGARIN'S 'set purpose' was set enough to keep him from Julia's side when she, her sister and Lord William FitzGerald made an expedition beyond the walls of Rome.

(It is in her note on this picture that Julia's great-niece wrongly calls Lord William Julia's step-father, as well as misunderstanding the picture's setting.)

Resolutely, Gagarin has stayed behind, in the Piazza Navona, where his lodgings are. His arms folded in pique, he sits on the convenient base of a pillar, in front of Bernini's fountain of the Four Rivers.

His mind's eye, however, has followed Julia, and the top of the picture shews his vision of the Taaffe-FitzGerald group on their expedition. Hills in the background, Roman walls to the right, they advance through a peasant crowd, making their way between a donkey-rider and a pair of minor ecclesiastics or monastics politicking.

Inevitably, Gagarin's imagination supplies a gentlemanly admirer who hurries forward to make Julia a deep bow.

As he visualises the expedition he has absented himself from, Gagarin wears on his face all the Byronic pride or sulk he can muster.

And on his left hand he wears a ring of a size not to be shamed even by the ecclesiastical jewellery of Rome.

Perhaps he is only shewing a Russian and princely taste for splendour. Yet he wears nothing of the kind in his other self-portraits, and the picture, destined for Julia, seems to draw it to her notice.

Perhaps it is a ring that Julia accepted from Gagarin and then, in her access of coldness or her disengagement from the destiny of the wild geese, returned?

15 *A Letter Aria*

I<small>T WAS</small> Gagarin's, not Julia's, resolution that broke.

In a summer night that is warm enough for the french window to stand open, under the full moon whose brilliancy in the blue night above Rome so regularly made, if not lovers, view-lovers sigh, he sits at his table in his rooms in Piazza Navona, in front of his inkwell and the reading lamp he had already sketched for her in his nonsense letter.

He writes her a letter, which she did not keep, and draws her a picture, which she did, of himself writing it.

Although the view from his window is Roman, and although with resolute unheroism he shews himself again in his braces, he has, perhaps to his detriment in Julia's now home-turning eyes, made it an intensely Russian scene.

Again, he seems to anticipate Tchaikovsky – this time in his conjunction with Pushkin. Gagarin might be one of the young officers, keeping late and worried solitary hours, in *The Queen of Spades*.

Or he might be a male Tatiana declaring in an impassioned aria-letter his luckless and unwanted love.

A fantasy Julia, again winged like a fairy or the ghost of a butterfly, has flown through the open window to offer him a Muse's inspiration.

Perhaps this phantasm of Julia is all he can now capture of the 'young man's dream' and the 'beautiful plan for the future'.

16 The End of the Story

J ULIA'S ANSWER to Gagarin's letter was a refusal to marry him.
Gagarin replied only by sending her the last of the drawings he did
for her. As a writer of nonsense fiction he had shewn a taste for quick
endings, though in real life he could not achieve a happy one.

Now it is he whose horses gallop out of Rome down an Appian Way –
this time the New Appian Way, which takes the same general direction as
the ancient one but through a different exit (the Porta San Giovanni) from
the city.

As they leave Rome and its gate on the hills behind them, a dialogue
passes between Gagarin and the companion he labels S. (for servant? or for
the name of a friend known to Julia?)

'Do you', asks S., trying to pick out landmarks, as travellers did and do
on approaching or leaving Rome, 'see Saint Peter's?'

Naming the street where Julia lodged, G. (Grégoire) replies:

'No, I see the Via del Babuino.'

His immediate destination is no doubt Naples, where he will take ship.
But his equipage is so quintessentially Russian, the passengers apparently
already muffled against the Russian frost though they are still in fact
traversing Italy in early summer, that you might think he was going to
drive on and on until he reaches St Petersburg.

17 Epilogue

GRIGORII Grigorievich Gagarin did indeed return permanently to St Petersburg from Italy in 1832.

There, suitably to the sympathy one of his drawings had shewn in advance, he became friends with Pushkin and, at Pushkin's request, illustrated his work. Perhaps he thought with irony of his picture of a mock duel when Pushkin was killed, in 1837, in a real one.

Gagarin married. His paintings include a portrait of his wife.

He pursued a career both as a visual artist and, after his father's example and in keeping with his family's relation to the Russian court, as a diplomatist-politician.

In the last two thirds of the 1830s he was sent on diplomatic missions to Munich and to Constantinople. He spent the 1840s in the Caucasus (where he became a friend of Lermontov, who was in exile there) taking part in the suppression of Georgian insurrection.

He drew and painted genre scenes in Russia and more exotic ones in Istanbul. Some of his work is now in the Russian Museum at Leningrad. From 1859 to 1872 he was vice-president of the Academy of Fine Arts at St Petersburg. He explored and wrote about Byzantine and early Russian archaeology.

He travelled both in Russia and in western Europe and died in 1893 at Châtellerault, France.

The sister who accompanied Julia to Rome never married – a statement that is true whether the sister concerned was indeed Martha or was Frances.

Julia, however, did marry.

Though she refused to follow the example of two of her siblings by taking a spouse from the Papal States, she did marry within the family sphere. In 1827, five years before Julia's visit to Italy, her second brother, Robert Taaffe (of Ardmulchan, Co. Meath, his maternal grandfather's property), had married the daughter of Theobald Mackenna (of Dublin).

The Theobald Mackenna whom Julia married was presumably a brother of her sister-in-law.

Thus Julia's marriage was Irish. Since, however, her husband was an Assistant Under-Secretary at Dublin Castle, the seat of Anglo-Irish administration, it could be said to be a strange marriage for an Irish patriot – though no stranger than Sarah Curran's to an English captain of artillery.

Julia bore a son, John Mackenna, and, as the genealogical books put it with their lack of interest in anything except primogeniture, 'other issue'. Her husband died in 1859. She herself lived till 1881.

The drawings Gagarin gave her in Italy in 1832 passed to the great-niece who wrote fragmentary notes to some of them. Perhaps Julia bequeathed them to her because as a child she had been so taken with them, though in that case it seems curious that the notes don't say so.

In annotating the pictures it was natural for the commentator to write of Julia Taaffe, since Taaffe was indeed Julia's surname at the time the pictures were drawn. It was equally natural that she should write of the sisters as Joanna and Julia Taaffe, since (whatever the problems of her first name) one of them retained that surname all her life.

Yet it is a little strange, in a context that emphasises family concerns, if not always accurately, that the notes never once speak of Julia Mackenna, the name Julia bore at the time when the writer of the notes knew her. No more does anyone speak of Sarah Curran as Sarah Sturgeon. Perhaps there was an unspoken sense in the family that Julia, too, had in some sort left her heart with a young hero, not in a grave but in St Petersburg.

In an introductory letter she prefaced to her notes, the commentator records: 'I can just remember her, a very old lady – & I was a very small child – she used to read fairy stories to me' (including, perhaps, the story as if for very small children that Gagarin had sent to Julia in Naples) '– & take me shopping in Dublin'. Julia, she says, 'lived to a very great age' (in fact, about 75).

The commentator writes of the charm of Gagarin's drawings. And of Julia she says: 'I can remember how charming she was – & how she spoilt me!'

Perhaps Julia was trying to pass on, along with the drawings, that spoilt child quality of hers that was a component of her charm and one that is preserved in the charm of Gagarin's not unsatirical drawings.

NOTE

I am extremely grateful to John Bayley for help he gave me; and to Michael Levey I owe deep thanks for help and advice of many kinds.

The books I have chiefly consulted are these. Lord Lewis Taaffe, 'present and ninth Viscount': *Memoirs of the Family of Taaffe*, not published, Vienna, 1856. Felix Mendelssohn Bartholdy: *Letters from Italy and Switzerland*, translated by Lady Wallace, Longman, 1864. Hector Berlioz: *Mémoires*, 1870, English translation 1937. *The Letters and Private Papers of William Makepeace Thackeray*, ed. Gordon N. Ray, Oxford U.P., 1945. *The Art of Russia 1800–1850, an exhibition from the museums of the USSR*, 1978, University of Minnesota, &c. *Allgemeines Lexikon der Bildenden Künstler,* ed. U. Thieme and F. Becker, Vol. XIII, 1920. *The Oxford Companion to Art,* ed. Harold Osborne, Oxford, 1970. *The Titled Nobility of Europe,* 1914. Burke's Irish Family Records, Burke's Peerage, Kelly's Handbook, various editions. Brian FitzGerald: *Emily Duchess of Leinster,* Staples Press, 1949. Mariana Starke: *Information and Directions for Travellers on the Continent,* 6th ed., 1828. Karl Baedeker: *Southern Italy and Sicily,* 1896. Herbert Weinstock: *Vincenzo Bellini,* Weidenfeld and Nicolson, 1971. Herbert Weinstock: *Donizetti,* Methuen, 1964. Elizabeth Longford: *Wellington: Pillar of State,* Panther, 1975. Joanna Richardson: *Stendhal,* Gollancz, 1974. John Brophy: *Sarah,* Collins, 1948.

B.B.